JOY
Comes in the Morning

Matthew A. Cooke

ISBN 978-1-63630-656-8 (Paperback)
ISBN 978-1-63814-508-0 (Hardcover)
ISBN 978-1-63630-657-5 (Digital)

Covenant Books, Inc.
11661 Hwy 707
Murrells Inlet, SC 29576
www.covenantbooks.com

Lovingly dedicated to
Matthew's friends and family,
especially his brother, Andrew,
and his daughters, Savannah and Allie

Heal me, O LORD, and I shall be healed; save me, and I shall be saved: for thou art my praise.

—Jeremiah 17:14 (KJV)

Contents

Part 5: Faith

Introduction

As we travel life's road, we have many valleys as well as mountaintop experiences. In this regard, my life has been no different than that of any other mother of sons. When my husband and I had our first child, we were elated. What a gift he was for us! From the moment we held him in our arms, he was a joy and delight. His was a normal childhood. I was a stay-at-home mom until he started kindergarten and I started my education once again. He was smart and always very mature for his age. We attributed this to his always being around adults and college students since his dad worked as a college professor and often took him to class with him. There was no reason for us to think he was going to head down a road that would lead to much sadness and disappointment, not only for us but also for himself.

Looking back on his young life, I now understand that his shyness and isolation at an early age was a sign of depression. He told me the first time he remembered the feeling of depression and not wanting to live was in the fifth grade. He always seemed happy to us; and his friends talked about what a clown he was at school, constantly making people laugh. Even today, when I see former classmates, they will talk about how funny and outgoing he was. They just never saw the tears, and neither did we until much later in life.

Matthew began drinking alcohol with his buddies when camping out on someone's farm at about sixteen. He didn't realize that would be the beginning of a lifetime of misery and heartache brought on by the addiction of alcohol and drugs. Early intervention may have steered him in a different direction, but his dad and I were once again uneducated and didn't know that the earlier one gets help for addiction, the greater the chance is to stop whatever the addiction may be. As time went on and he became an adult, his unhappiness and troubles became greater and out of control. No matter how much we or his brother tried to help him, it was to no avail.

After many stays in recovery facilities and months of sobriety, he would always go back to the destructive behavior. Even through these difficult days, Matthew never lost his faith in God. He believed very strongly that Jesus, as his Heavenly

Father, loved him and wanted what was best for him. He never failed to tell other people what God had done for him and how he was blessed. He witnessed to those he knew and didn't know. He set an example in this respect much greater than we did.

Matthew began writing when he was a very young child. The first thing he wrote was when he was nine years old. He would often bring me something he had written and ask me to read it to see what I thought and ask me to type it for him. Through the years, he continued to write. You can see in his writings his love for God, family, friends, and nature, but also his despair and sadness. I typed what he brought me, but unfortunately many of his things were lost through the years.

After he lost his battle with his demons on November 3, 2019, I found more of his handwritten work that I had not read before. This put me on a quest to share his story. I feel his work can be both uplifting in seeing his faith through his trials and give hope to those who suffer from addiction and depression. I pray this compilation of his works will let you see the son we knew and loved, for very few really knew him.

Matthew's days on earth seem so short. His dad and I will always treasure the years we had with him. We will miss him until we see him in glory.

His Mother,
Wanda Cooke

PART 1

Family and Love

My First Love, My Mama

In my mind's eye, there is a face that shines upon me.
It has guided my days since I first saw creation. There
　　exists a bond so pure that it begins before life on
　　earth.
Your hair is like wisteria as it wipes the tears from
　　my eyes.
Your cradling touch is that of an earthen angel.
O, how I shall always crave it.

You know my heart so well, my senses constantly
　　search for you. The thoughts I have seem to be
　　known by you before I even utter them. God
　　wove me inside you, it was you who gave me
　　life. Time nor distance, grief nor pain can sep-
　　arate my heart from yours.

You personify what a woman of God should be. A
　　pulsating that beats of two; the wonders of one
　　is the wondering of the other. A pure divine
　　unity in God's world.

You were playmate and friend when there was no
other.

To be consoled by your touch, your hug, your kiss,
or the sweet perfume of words from your
mouth; could in an instance put me at ease. I
reminiscence in the depths of your soul, bathed
in tranquility by your goodness and the beating
of your heart.

Matthew

Daddy, Come Find Me

The tears that stain my face fall from the well of joy
that ripples inside me when my thoughts turn
to you, Dad.

The cobwebs deliquesce from my mind; I begin to
break the cocoon of my slumber.

Cool breezes of the mountain morning and you, at
the griddle, greet your son as he peeks through
the zipper of the world.

Magic creek water ignites my world; I bask in a
swimming hole of love and reminiscence.

Fireflies light the path of my dreamscape; songs of
the hills fill the air as we share our souls over ice
cream made by Marge.

As long as the waves break, streams babble in their
beds, tires sing upon our highway...till Zion is
cast in shadows, the steam dissipates from the
"Ole Faithful One," the electricity is turned off
outside Topeka...

While pitching wedges still hit close on the South
Carolina hole, and the Chimney Tops still daz-
zle us in the morning...

Through rocky mountain days, clear canyon nights,
    and afternoons at the jetty…
I will forever be the "sunshine on your shoulders."
"Oh, Daddy, come find me!"
What sweet words…
I love you,

                                    Your son,
                                    Matthew

To My Best Friend

Paper dissolves the power of my words; ink gives them no credence.

The spoken word is blown away like sand, leaving only the rhythm of my heart to proclaim my adoration for you.

I crept into the blush of the world as a special gift from God.

My fragility and wonder began on your chest. My lungs filled with yours as one. I was edified at your knee, learning to talk and run, laugh, and love.

Oh, how I loved...my romance with the world began with you.

The anthems of my youth hailed from your heart, your soul, your lips, filling my heart with sweet surrender.

The most consequential cornerstone for my life was laid by your caressing hands.

The mirror soothes me to my midst; I conjure the
    face that is so dear to me from the image I see.
My future unfolds before me, I see a vision of what
    is to come...

"How shall a Christian man treat his wife?" asked
    my son. "What should his character reveal?
    Where should Jesus resurface in his life?"
"My son," I reply, "I can grant you the answers, only
    because they were personified in the actions of
    my Father."

Love,
Matthew
To his Dad
2001

My Family

Never worry, never fret that I'm not little "Rich
Man Bret."

I love and am proud of who I am the boy of Wanda
and Tom and son of Uncle Sam.

We are never ashamed of what we have or who we
are, for we now have bought Mom a brand-
new car.

Yes, yes, yes, it's true! There are no parents as loving
as you.

You are the best, the best who never want to rest
for their two boys, who fill their lives with fun
and joy!

Yes, I love you, Mom and Dad, you're the best I
could have ever had.

I love you,
Matthew
1986

The Hat

I was rummaging through a chest one day when I
    happened upon an old cowboy hat.
It was rough and torn, shabby all about; it had been
    made of beaver. Yes, I remember all that.
There I sat on the floor holding this hat, wondering
    where the boy was who had worn it all flat.
Flashes and glimpses came to my mind. There was a
    saffron-haired boy smiling and cute, just happy
    to be there wearing it that day.
The adventures he had scampered about in my
    head; it was sweet memories of a time far away.
He rode high on his saddle attached to a stick. He was
    gallant and true, fearless and bright; however, I
    knew that is not how he'd stay.
The sheriffs in town, his Mom and Dad, looked to
    him with fondness and all the love that they had.
That young cowpoke was the light of their life.
    They had no way of knowing that his future
    would be so sad.
He thought, just as they, his days were secured,
    always to be honest, happy, and glad.
Yet, alas! That cowboy grew up. He began to ramble
    down a pathway of sin; his once bright future
    became so cosmically dim.

The years passed away, wasted in time. Loneliness and darkness stood in his way, and his choices became colossally slim.

Thirty years later, kneeling on this floor, tears flowed freely from a heart that was torn; I realized now as I should have then that the only way back would be to turn to Him.

He who through death brought back the true light. He who gave us a will to do right.

Standing up tall after saying my prayer, I put back on my hat and turned to God's sight.

Matthew

Playground

Thousands of footprints litter my past, straying
far and wide over a world known only to my
memory.

I swam in an ecosystem of friends, games, and
familiarity; the lives of that kindred age stay
with me even until this day.

Laughter floated on autumn breezes as footballs
were passed, kicked, and fumbled; knees were
skinned, and muscles were bruised in a Gaelic
dance of youthful triumph.

Secrets and oaths were passed between the warriors
of my childhood; each so grave, so honest, so
eternally binding.

The future was a lifetime away, yet as near as the
next field of grass that beckoned us to its ripe-
ness with the secret essence of boyhood.

Our heroes played on landscaped acres that were
homogeneous to the backyard ballparks, where
records were chased and legends were made.

In this age of such sweet innocence, *teammate* meant
a bond of brotherhood that seemed ceaseless
and never-ending, where secret plays and coded

words were whispered in breathless homage to our game.

On golden soaked summer days, where dusk came late and darkness was never late enough, I floated in an enchantment that belongs only to childhood and can only be remembered but never recaptured.

I am old now, but sometimes I see a glimpse of a moment, the boy I was; ball in hand, a gleam in his eye, and a dream that one day he would be a man of reckoning.

This Is Love

I have seen snow glitter like fine silk on the Colorado
mountainside casting reflections that could
blind a man's eye.

The skies of the desert have opened up to me like
a dark maiden, revealing her billion stars that
stretch from horizon to horizon.

I have caught the sun cresting the Atlantic, rising
like a fireball, transforming the tides into a crim-
son procession that swims endlessly toward me.

The thick white fog of the Smoky Mountains has
immersed me in its arms as I laid among her
magnificent foliage of spring.

Yes, God is so mysterious in His ways and His time,
for He waited many years to reveal His most
beautiful creation.

When He allowed me to finally gaze on your face, I
realized how it must feel for a mortal to look an
angel in the eyes.

To my daughter, my first born

Love

What can one say about a love that is lost? Was there ever love? Surely there must have been! The feelings of love still flow and ebb like the tides through my veins, through my soul. Is it better to have loved and lost than to never have loved at all? I have pondered this question over and over and can only come up with the summation that I would rather have loved than not. In fact, in my consciousness, in my heart, and in the recesses of my soul, I know that I have an infinite need for love!

I have found through deep self-analysis that it is not being alone that frightens me. I, one soul and body, was tendered to this earth alone; and I, like others, will depart from this spaceship we call earth alone. I fully accept these undeniable laws because as humans we agreed to live simply because we were thrown here from above. Yet as a thinking, feeling, delicate human being, I have an unquenchable need and desire to give and receive the affections, feelings, trust, understanding, and yes, love that is received and given to and from one human being to another.

My heart bleeds sweet nectar. I ache deep in the very bowels of my being for a love, for a feeling, for a moment in time that was missed and is now gone forever. Though I still am, though I still think, feel, wonder, and live my life to the fullest that I may, there will remain an emptiness inside me. I can fill my mind with knowledge. I am able to teach and touch people in a way many cannot, and this pleases me. God granted me a multitude of gifts and talents, and for that, I am grateful beyond words and give praise to Him. I have locked inside of myself so many thoughts, emotions, dreams, and memories; but the keys to my soul, to my heart, are intricate and laden with doubt and shame. My soul—me— so wants to let these wonders, gifts, emotions, joy, and love combust through my flesh and my mouth so they may soothe another, thereby soothing me!

Being human, we are also animals with some of the same instincts of our furry cousins. Though we share many innate traits with our four-legged friends, we as humans have been given the cognitive power to differentiate between primal sex and lust. This is where my heart and mind disseminate: it is not the sex I desire but the sharing of feelings, friendship, trust, respect, and love that binds man to woman and woman to man in an ecstasy of appreciation, understanding, and eventually a monogamy of carnal knowledge of each other that will be much more than sex—it will be love in the most natural of physical forms that only those who are in love can display.

> Though I speak with the tongues
> of men and angels, and have not love,
> I become as sounding brass, or a tin-
> kling cymbal. And, though I have
> the gift of prophecy, and understand
> all mysteries, and all knowledge; and
> though I have all faith, so that I could
> move mountains, and have not love,
> I am nothing. And though I bestow
> all my goods to feed the poor, and
> though I give my body to be burned,
> and have not love, it profits me
> nothing. Love suffers long and is
> kind; love envies not; love vaunteth
> not itself, it is not puffed up. It does
> not behave itself unseemly, seeks
> not her own, is not easily provoked,
> and thinks no evil. Rejoices not in

iniquity, but rejoices in truth; bears all things, believes all things, hopes in all things, endures all things. And now abide by faith, hope, and love, these three; but the greatest of these is *love*! (1 Cor. 13, emphasis mine)

Sounds for an Angel

Imagine if you can...
>   rain falling on the tin roof of our cabin; the
>   drops of rain are my fingers lovingly tapping
>   a song onto your head.

Imagine if you can...
>   a mountain stream cascading over rocks in
>   its unstoppable journey to the sea; the down-
>   ward flow is like my hands passing down the
>   length of your body.

Imagine if you can...
>   a thunderstorm rolling over the flowing
>   plains; the rumbles you feel from the heavens
>   are like the trembling of two lovers that have
>   been united.

Imagine if you can...
>   the breaking waves of the ocean, crumbling
>   down upon the earth; the crashes are the
>   sound of two hearts beating in unison for a
>   love that has opened.

Imagine if you can...
>   the sound of my telling you that I love you.

That, my girl, is the sound of a man in love.

The Dance

It was always so easy, so natural, like a rainbow in
   the mist.

You and I entangled in time.

O, how you lighted upon me like a dove sent from
   Zion. Like the breath of a graceful flower, you
   filled my senses.

You let me love you, adore you, and feel your love;
   almost celestial was our road to each other. It was
   so simple then yet so hard to comprehend. Our
   extraordinary dance began on a lake of glass.

Laughter filled the ears of angels when our eyes
   met and our bodies brushed together; music of
   joy guided our steps as we twirled in the dawn
   of our destiny.

The sweetest feeling I knew was being alone with
   you; the smallest of gestures made me dream
   of a love that was inconceivable pre-you. Love
   was why I came to you in the first place. Love
   for you is why I danced.

Ever changing are the seasons of our heart, a con-
   tinuum based not on time but rather on desires
   of a spiritual plane. The stars in the heavens

can attest to our dance; it will be there as a constellation of our adoration.

Our lake has turned brackish now as tears flood my world; the music has died somehow; I stand alone on the dance floor.

Where was my misstep? Where did I lose the rhythm we had?

I spiral down through the silver clouds to find my partner has left me.

The why and how will be forever disguised; now I wait by a wall of somber blackness to be swept away once again in *the dance*.

PART 2

Nature

A Twig

A twig fell from the branch of a mighty tree that
    grew upon the edge of a brook.
The twig knew not why it fell, or when, or what the
    reason was for.
The twig landed in the streaming brook, and just to
    its dismay, it saw the tree, her home, growing
    far away.
The little twig was wet and cold as it floated away.

Birth

The warm, salty breeze caresses my face as I stare into the darkness.

My skin shivers as dampened droplets converge on my soul.

Though my senses tingle with the feelings of life, I see only nothingness.

My feet are planted, submerged in the moistness of creation.

My ears are filled with muffled rumblings from depths unseen.

I feel the push, the surge, the power; I sense the urgency.

The Mother heaves her waves of anguish across the contours of her body.

The sizzling scream of the Mother's passion deafens me.

My other senses come alive to behold the cresting of her sun above the horizon.

I have seen the birth of a new day in all its miraculous glory, and I will stand in these same sands to watch its death.

How glorious though is the time in between!

Cat Tails

Tonight, I sleep…for a while anyway.

It's hard to sleep all night. There are situations which must be addressed, conditions that beg my attention.

So I jump from my bed and pad around my abode to be sure all is as it should be.

Noises and stray lights are scrutinized carefully.

I can't let the least miscreants escape my opaque eyes.

Finally, I am satisfied, so I clean and find the place I decided to sleep again. I sleep, I eat, and I am loved.

That is all I know… I am a cat.

To my good friend, Sylvia

Love,
Matthew

Footprints

I walk across a tidal beach for miles and miles and
    miles.
When I looked back from whence I came, I saw
    only slick, wet sand.
The unity was perfect; nothing broke or impeded
    its smooth delicacy.
So I stood still, gazing across where I roamed.
I then prudishly looked down to the sand between
    my toes.
I knew I was here, could feel the sand beneath my
    feet, the wind in my hair; hear the waves break-
    ing in my ears.
There was no doubt about the direction I had strode
    though there was scantily a trace.
No one could follow me here or learn from my
    expedition.
Nothing behind me signified great achievement,
    except that I was here.
Here, where I will be found, mourned, and forgotten.
O, Lord, what a waste of a beautiful beach.

Morning Delight

As the sun outlines the eastern mountains, he glides into the cold flowing waters. Footsteps in the fog over the water give the mystical feeling of men long ago.

It is this time of day that can take hold of a man. Mysteries are unfolded before him; enlightenment ascends on a mind set free by a virginity of time and space.

Moving through the dawn of creatures engulfed in rapids and rocks, he seeks stoically to find the flawless place where his world will meet theirs.

The white spray of a river crying touches his face; the eddies of deepness shows her sadness, and the splash of life bubbling her surface reveals the delight of her secret.

Armed only with rod and fly, a four-movement dance of sweet harmony simultaneously begins as rays of gold lick her hurried surface.

A void of un-remembrance conceals all but thirty feet of line that is laid out in jubilation and in quest, pursuing gifts of life that are given only to those who believe in the magic of her waters.

The transformation of a man is made when he connects with the water; he has become one with the enigma she beholds—he becomes the embodiment of the universe.

In a cocoon of joyous fascination, he works his rod, conducting an orchestra of nature's finest adornments, swaying in a tempo of life that is found on the highest planes of peace and serenity.

The alms she hides in her rock-laden bed are given only to the just and the patient; for to lure a child of the river, to lay hold of her offspring, is but a fleeting moment of ecstasy—yet one that will stay etched into your soul for eternity.

A fisherman takes, but he returns. The mark he makes is upon himself. The gift is his for a lifetime; the magic is left behind to remain for the next trackless soul who wonders to her shores with rod and fly and wonder.

Matthew

River

Does a brook decide to diverge for a portion of it
   to take a separate path?
Or is the separation preplanned, destined before
   the first drop rolled down its dried bed?
Does the water get a voice as to what route it takes?
Or is it chance, a map of fate written before the
   winds of time?
Once I flowed east with all of me intact. Now I flow
   divided with parts of myself separated.
Intimacies and loves that I once knew so well are
   now but mercy clouds of memory.
Yes, my world is now divided, and I know not what
   to do.
Part of me flows on east; the rest flows away with you.

Matthew

Sea

I feel slow rumbling deep within me, it leaves chills
on my body and shudders in my soul.

The deep of the sea swells up in catastrophic
explosions, leaving the surface in a mad frolic
of ecstasy.

The waves of my emotions surge forward, leaving
nothing in its wake; the voyage is one of destiny, guided only by the moon.

The arc of its destination is in fantasy, not in sight,
with the building of expectation it crests to its
highest height.

The golden coast it does see now, glimmering just
within reach. I want to reach the pinnacle of
my crescendo before I reach the sun-drenched
beach.

I break and crash down onto the shores of your
loveliness, leaving pieces of me upon you in
foams of white.

I have given all I can give, and now I ebb away!

Stream

Cool and clear, she flows as she has forever, shim-
mering, rippled, full of life and wonder.

She shapes the world around her, carving her unique
signature for all to see, to know, to love.

Like the tears of a fair maiden pulled by gravity,
signifying the feelings of the earth, she streaks
the surface and bares her soul.

Touching all who wander to her shores with words
of contemplation and comfort, she sings her
endless hymn of praise.

Cleansed by the mist of her surface, I plunge to the
womb of her depths, kept safe by the tides of
her tenderness.

Matthew

"The Great Smoky Mountains," My Happy Place

It might seem impossible to hide from the air...

However, it's been done; and when it seems you are finally totally hidden, boys simultaneously awaken in a land of smoke and magic.

This is a place that exists both in God's world and in the minds and hearts of little boys' worlds.

An enraptured place, where there are fireflies to light the emerging dusk, where each sound made and each sight sought is captivating as well as titillating.

In the accommodation, where all colors are the kaleidoscope of a fairy tale landscape, battles have been fought by small green men, as well as brown-shouldered boys.

A place where adventure and consternation can instantaneously be found around the next bend.

A place where satellites are hunted among the constellations, making their anticipated rendezvous with four awestruck eyes.

A place where brothers fall in love with each other, with family, with life, with God, and yes, with girls.

This is a void where the washing machine always works, where "Aiken Drum" plays uninterrupted upon his ladle, and *whimmy-diddle* is still an enchanted word.

I am a very old place; but I still remember those two gingerbread, golden-haired children who warmed my water with their hearts and tickled the air with their laughter. Lest they never forget, and may they always be APPROACHING ELKMONT.

Love,
Matthew

The Shore of Life

A utopia of bright pastels and dark hues surround
me. The iridescent sea cries for me in the mourn-
ful tone of a lioness searching for her lost cub.
Soft sand made for the bed of the deliquesce shell
of sea turtles run for miles while raptors skim,
hover, and soar.
The unyielding breeze cooling or warming with the
seasons bend the oats in an eternal perpendic-
ular dance.
The damp aroma of sand, salt, fish, and seaweed
engulfs my senses. Here I feel alive; for life sur-
rounds, consumes, and makes my heart weep
gleefully.
Foam tickles my toes as I become the dancer in an
oceanic ballet that belongs to me and her alone.
I encounter immense, glorious life, as well as
unavoidable death, as they run concurrently
strewn along where her water recedes.
The moon and the sun kiss her caps with their own
distinguished but not less adoring love.

As a trustful soul mate, she will always be there, reminding me of my mortality but also the undying pleasures of life.

You speak to me with words that have been spoken forever. I speak to you with awe and affection in my heart.

You, just as I, were created to serve; and you are unyielding in your dazzling duties. Let me learn from you; let me never quit but keep coming to shore even when I am rebuked again and again by barriers of sand and rock.

Darling, you harbor billions of scores of life; they live within you and nourish from you. I, also, have One living in me that is mightier than your blue whale—that is the Holy Spirit, and His agape for me is unfathomable.

Your ebbs and flows are never ending; your works are sure and pertinent. Without you, I would not be. Your depths are a mystery; as are mine. They may be explored but only so limitedly.

What are we hiding? What is at our bottom? Will we ever know? Yes, when we reach the shores of our heavenly home. Praise be to God!

PART 3

Sufferings

Abyss

Slipping, sliding, falling, perilously close to the edge.
The abyss looms like a gaping wound before me.
My perception is skewed; I am void of reality.
Vertigo overwhelms me, spinning my soul.
Space and time convulse and twist into a kaleido-
　　scope of meaningless abstraction.
My fear is unyielding; it will not abate.
I pray only for a dreamless slumber, a place of peace
　　and tranquility.
A dimension where love envelopes me, and I fear
　　no more… Forever!

Dream

I sink into my consciousness, alone, stranded, with
nowhere to hide.

The leviathan of it is startling. It pulses, it is unkempt,
it drags down with a force that is unwavering
and mighty.

I cannot see there, nor do I want to. But I feel...
Oh, yes, I feel.

The reality of this interspace is horrifically breath-
taking, my lungs deflate, I suffocate.

I hear the outside world. It screams at me, it laughs
at me, it cries for me.

The waterfall of eternity embraces my soul, crashes
over it with a mighty force.

I am drenched with the sweat of the sufferer. I
shake with the fear of the condemned.

My cries are not heard through the dreary fog of my
imprisonment.

I have no reprieve from my fate; I am bound by the
chains of the insane.

The freedom I seek looms like a rainbow—it is
beautiful yet always out of reach.

Glory

Night, night, come to me with the grandeur you offer as alms for those able to hear.

O, night, night, leave me now. Release me from your delicate web. I have been your confidant, your companion, your slave ad infinite.

Your beauty no longer stimulates; your aesthetics have demised. My eyes do not reflect your magnificent allure. You betrayer of souls, get thee behind me, and let the light make its triumphant return.

The wonder of your celestial bodies is hidden from my sight; instead, I run blindly through a battlefield of abysmal death.

How I yearn to see a sliver of light from the east. But alas, I search in vain. You hide from me, oh, darkness, with your demonic claws and sulfuric breath the life I can have in the light.

I hear and crave the voices of those who love me; I vaguely feel their touch. I fall mortified past them. Though they are obstructed by gloom, let them always see me for the person God made me to be.

Oh, Lord, I am crippled by life; a plethora of hell
    hounds sense my emptiness. Save me!
Lost in fear, forgotten in a labyrinth of self-loath-
    ing, I grovel for a reprieve. I aguishly pray for
    this chalice to be taken from me.

Matthew
2007

My Cry unto Thee

My battle cries are eternal. They resound in an intimacy that belongs only to me. To let them rage against the world would stand me up against the one I dread the most—myself.

I convulse at conformity. Blackened lids steer me clear of conscious righteousness; scar tissue constricts what might be my resolve to normalize.

I navigate the undulation of this psychedelic world masquerading as a clown. My hopes of acceptance fall in a lava lamp of misrepresentation and fraud.

The cringing of a life fallen stands before me like a Greek statue. There is no restitution that can be done—no tearing down, no building up. I am mortified.

Hope gathers around me in a mist of moderation, calamity, strife, and soul; scorching fears burn away what dreams engulf me. I am a prisoner of agony.

Curse be the pleas of my pleading! Damnation falls upon me like a rock; scourge and retribution follow me to my actualization as a man. I am less, Lord. I am less.

I cast the net of my life into the living sea of God, hoping to find courage and redemption. Though the nets pull heavy, they bulge with anger, fear, and recrimination.

My sobs are eternally exploding. To vent would be to tear the flesh of my wounds. Expose them for the cowardice that they are. How can one stand less than a man?

Let loose this mighty torrent. Give way to the river of rage. Let free the spirit of the man You chose. Cleanse him with the breath of Your mouth.

Hiding is my way, O, Lord. Now, today, let Your magnificent grace free me of my bondage to this world of trickery and faultiness.

Beckon me to You as I turn from the world of the dying, seeking refuge from my hate, to culminate in the forgiveness and love of Your bosom.

My Dearest Love

I realize it has not been very long since you heard from me, but I felt it necessary to write you this letter. I admit fully from the start that it has been very hard for me to have the fortitude to write this to you, and it's probably going to be hard for you to hear. However, because of where I am in my life, it is something we are both just going to have to accept and deal with.

Do you remember when we first met? I was very young, and when I found you, it was literally love at first sight. You instantly made me feel like the complete person I always wanted to be. Yes, those were the good ole days! We spent weekends together and had so much fun. It was so exciting and glamorous; you gave me self-esteem, courage, and prestige—all the things I thought I lacked.

As we grew up, you and I started spending our time more exclusively together. The days and nights were still enjoyable and carefree, but you started to hinder my other relationships and responsibilities (though then I did not see it). As years went by and we became impregnable and insep-arable, most of my time and money were going to you. It was then that others saw what I did not—I idolized you; I worshiped the ground you walked on.

Upon reflection, it is these circumstances in our relationship that started to change. Even though I loved you and entirely gave myself to you, you began to turn on me. I was blind to your coor-dinated ambush, but as I look back, I can now see when you started really leading me astray. I would lie for you and feel no remorse. I would steal for you and not fear any personal retribu-tion. You were so cunningly sly and convincing; I was eating out of the palm of your persuasive hand.

As you well know, by this time, I was 100 percent consumed by you. There was nothing of me that I would not give, nothing I would not do, just by a simple plea from you in my ear. You went from lover to archenemy overnight, and I was your hostage. We both share the same memories from that time to this, so I feel no need to rehash then all here. I will, however, remind you of what you stole from me. You took my integrity, honesty, and values. You took my friends, my family members, and wives. You took my humanity, my goodness, my faith, and finally my health. You took it all, and I loathe you for it.

I am telling you now inexplicably that I am severing all ties with you. I now finally have the affirmation, the faith, and the guts to tell you I want you out of my life forever. If you call me, I will not answer my phone. If you knock on my door, I will leave it closed and bolted. I know that will not matter to you; I realize you will stalk me from the shadows until the end of my days. But I give you fair warning: from now on, I will be surrounded by a network of supporters that will be there to help me fight you. You will not find me in the company of the same people and same places as you did before. I am from now on going to wrap myself in a cocoon of protection that is called recovery. I will have people, and most of all, I will have God to help me avoid you forevermore.

So no good-byes. No looking behind. Just go and good riddance to you forever.

No longer yours,
Matthew

(This letter shows how strong the pull of addictions are. Matthew fought this battle for many years.)

Past

The seasons of life change before us; they do not wait. We must grasp hold of what we can before it slips away into obliqueness.

Transition is our duty; it falls upon our watch. We must be steadfast and observant to glean all there is to see.

Ours is the keeper of time; it falls upon our path. Whatever is left is left for eternity—only the kept can be treasured.

Today is but a blur, the future an unknown mystery; yesterday is all we have to learn from, to judge, to love.

O, but can we have what we seek? Is there a way to save the evermore of our past? Our brains sift through granules of time, so much is lost and scattered beyond our relocations.

All that we have is fleeting; we shall not be ourselves on the morrow.

Human life takes what cannot be reimbursed; the gradual erosion of memory is self-evident.

Our plunge into the future is done blindly. Promises
have not been pledged; our very life swings on a
pendulum that may never pass back before us.

So today I commit to memory, living it like it 'twas
the last. I will learn all I can and leave the rest
to time.

If tomorrow, therefore, decides to raise its mighty
head, I shall be ready or completely incapac-
itated, depending on what I cultivated from
today.

Today is my only chance.

Pathways

Lines have been crossed, and paths have been
  explored; a wanderer's way searches but never
  finds his vital store.

Some trails have led to goodness while others led to
  pain; most though have led only to soul-hurting
  bane.

Trudging through what is the swampland of my
  life, I find I cannot see what is wrong and what
  is right.

I fear every shadow, and I know not which road to
  take; I reel with impotence with every limping
  step I light.

My guide has lost me in the misty fog of life.

I walk so unsteady now though nothing is in my way.

Up and down I slither on the slide of life. The only
  place I want to be is someplace sure, happy, and
  nice.

Sometimes the journey stops off, and it is there I
  regain my head.

I look around at all God's things and find that I am
  blessed despite what I have said.

The torture though continues into nights as black as dark; many, many times, I feel that I fall oh so very short.

I thrash around in solitude, skittish of every thought, not wanting to be alone but fearing to be a part.

Gifts and talents fall wasted to the sides of where I pass; I find no way to harvest them, much less to make them last.

The frigid air of winter blows through me in late June; icicles of my past imprison me in shame and entomb.

I wake to find me weeping, and I sleep to make it stop; miseries and miracles encircle my every day, but I make no move to stop them. I just let them lay.

I see me on my deathbed many moons from now.

O, what sweet sorrow it will bring me somehow.

Lying there with my convictions, my loves, my losses, my hates; there it is! My path will end with just one dying date.

How will I be judged in life? Will it be by what I should have done or by the very pretty thoughts I sat there and spun for fun?

My death will come with great regret to friend and foe alike; for I, they know, have lived my life

without the great goodbye, never having left my mark on a life that should have shone.
Yea, with all life's trials behind me at the end, at last I pray this quiet little prayer as I let out my last gasp and say:

> "Forgive me, oh, Lord of heaven, take this sinner in, trim the bark from his sides that kept the true him in. Let the light of Christ finally rise through his pureness, and give him grace and mercy; for he is now truly yours." Amen.

Play

The play of life twists around me in a continuous
    melee of happiness and hate.
A tragic comedy unfolding before me, the direc-
    tor unseen, unheard, yet in total control of the
    production.
Its cast of characters know their lines, hit their
    marks, then recede from the spotlight into the
    dimness of the netherworld.
I remain on the stage hoping only to perform my
    best, not knowing the life span of my character.
Will I remain for the curtain call? Shall I last till
    the final encore? Will my bow be long and gaily
    received?
I know not the outcome of this script. I can only
    pray for Serenity, engulf myself in the act, and
    seize each morsel of life upon the stage.

Reality

How can this be reality? Where is the goodness, the hope, the sense of self, God's manifest destiny for me? I do not know where to turn or where to go. My shell is translucent; I cannot hide from the demons that swarm around my soul in their mad flight of fury and joy. They are confiscating my character, my being.

My beacons are insignificant while the world flows around. I flounder in an endless tide of apologies and retribution.

Flames from a dimension that is not of this world cloud my mind and skew my judgement; they burn me from all sides. Where shall I turn?

I dream the same dream every night. The sweat and chills wake me from a landscape of dark, morbid consequences. Save me from that reality! How can I overcome? Is there any chance for the 'morrow, or is it as it seems? Am I in an oblivion of unreality, where there is no escape, no surrender? I need lifting up. I need the strings of the puppet master. The quagmire of my life runs down my face into a putrid facsimile of my life here; I cannot ingest all there is to do, see, be responsible for. My emotions run down a turbulent stream of uncertainty and confusion; madness is my confidant. It drives down the avenue of self-delusion and doubt; my mind is a psychedelic chessboard. Visions of colossal doom dance before my eyes. My shadow mocks me. All pathways are dead ends. A tidal wave of sorrow topples me to my knees. I lie breathless on the sands of my life. I sprint forward in reverse, all edges are jagged, and there is no shortcut. My master calls to me from his glass castle. His amber mote drowns my soul. I cannot breathe. Walk with me now into the tomb of the burned and the ravished. Glean what the fire makes of mere mortals.

The Deceiver

Hello there, you adorable you. Today is the day of your destiny. I have so much to tell you. The enormity of your future is now at hand.

Do I have your attention? Can you feel your confidence in me bloom inside of you? Yes, that is what you need to do. Let go. Let me whisper sweet nothings to you for a time.

O, you, poor soul, what has happened to your life? Where are your dreams, your riches, your fame? Can you tell me where it all went wrong?

It's okay to cry and scream out your vengeance unto this unfair world. You have a right to be vexed. You have been led astray by all who supposedly loved you.

Ah, but cry no more, for I am here! And I have what you have been yearning for. Relax; let my silver tongue tell you the wondrous truths you have so hopelessly longed for.

Listen and do it well, for I am the "father of the air." Do not give in to guilt or remorse, for what good are they to you? Seek what pleasures you want, for that is all you are here to do.

What good is there to being kind and gentle when the rewards you reap serve only to keep you from what is rightfully yours? Do not be a fool, my love.

Seek your heart, your thrills. Throw all caution to the wind. Do not let something as loathsome as ethics or truth detain you from your every whim. Plunder the world, for it belongs to you; and I shall always be there to render my service.

Take without asking, speak but never listen, and do with no regard for others. These are your keys to ecstasy. Be brash about their usage, be unrelenting, be selfish! Only then will this kingdom of earth be yours.

Pluck now this sweet fruit. Let the juices of pleasure run down your face. Lick the nectar of proud victory from your golden fingers.

O, dear one, believe in yourself and yourself alone, for there is no one higher. Give credence to this truth I speak; and one day, my child, we will walk through the gates of eternity together, forever. I promise.

From,
The Evil One

The End

The end has come my love…

END. What an ugly word. Three letters that have been randomly arranged to symbolize a stopping point.

All forms, feelings, ideas, and hopes are final at the end.

Oh! How so, do I cling to thee with the ferocity of a black angel being flung, rejected by your infamy.

For whose lightless light is a beacon for the broken, the lame, and the helpless.

Tales of strife, pain, love, hate, and joy have been sung, written, and have even lived among you.

Oh, but 'tis the flight of a monarch, the blush of a kiss from a maiden, that seems unlimited never to die.

But there…always there… The end.

The Worm and Me

Part 1

I watched a worm crawl one day; it went here, there, near everywhere really. Though not pleasing to the eye, somehow, I was transfixed by its wiggling ways. I played pleasurably with its actions. Controlling the worm came to no small affair. Time elapsed around with its contortions. The worm grew and grew through the motions that I put him through. He became quite intolerable to handle. Through no negotiable way, the worm through its play, pierced and entered me. I felt his glee as he traveled though me, seeing what there was to see. Oh, the potential he saw, the paradisiacal places we could go together. As he flowed through my life blood from my heart to my brain, we knew what we could do together.

Love,
Me

Part 2

Now, I must at this juncture tell you the sights, the sensations, the untold pleasures I've had; and I owe it wholly, justifiably, and particularly to him. We have had ecstasies of unworldly physicalities. We have achieved a bliss, an extinctual nirvana that so few have had. Together I have fended off pain, stayed far from the remorseful place of reality. What I have accomplished is a zone of such inexistence that nothing else matters but me. I rule this world of the magically beautiful; all I need now is more time. That is the trick to my alchemistic allusion. I need time, time, more time. Please pleasure me, nourish me.

Sincerely,
The Worm

Time

The current of time sweeps me away. I fight, but it
makes no difference to time.

The winds of change swoon and swoop, taking
with it all who dwell on the landscapes of life.

The tailwinds of my past are unchangeable. They
serve only to propel me to a destiny of what I
don't know.

I can only float on their tides praying that they
land me softly on my future, which is seconds
and eons away.

Though the headwinds are fierce, they do not
stall my birth into the future—they only mud-
dle its perception.

I cannot foretell what is to come, nor can I explain
what has happened. All I know is that I am now,
in this second, in this morsel of time.

I am haunted by the air around me.

What

What I see brings no real surprise; it is there always, unchanging before me.

It is the unseen, the blackness that lies beyond, that tears charity from my heart.

What I hear in this world brings no revelation, no sense of foreboding or joy. It is the haunting taunts from another dominion that bring me to my knees.

What I feel has no relevance in this realm of existence, for what I feel transcends the veneer of this three-dimensional world of delusion.

What is tangible exists not in this world; to touch is only an illusion of a mind that is skewed to trick you into believing what is real.

What is there to taste if it is only bitter to your tongue? It is better to live in hunger than to consume the false hope of deliciousness that can never be found.

What is to say when all has been said? It is futile to try and give credence to false hopes and ideas through echoing your voice in silence to an unhearing future.

What gives directions, gives misdirections, if the path you follow is an abomination?

How will I know? Could I change? Or as I suspect, does it matter not?

Where the winds blow, I cling to go; it matters not of its final destination. I will be only in another locality where my senses are invalid.

I traverse this earth not knowing or seeing, not hearing or speaking, not tasting or touching. I pass through—that is all—unable to do more.

Lost in the limbo of reality, deemed mad by fellow journeyers, I continue on hoping in vain to find another spirit such as I.

In a world that is lost, I drift muddled in its womb, each day giving new hope that I shall be reborn into the world of the found.

Words

Words are all I have.

How do you live on words?

People are foreign to me because they do not understand my words.

I speak, but it is a silent echo.

I move, but it is like a shadow on a cloudy day.

I yell for the Lord, but my voice seems to stifle in my throat.

I turn to the ones I love, but I seem to turn the wrong way.

Beleaguered, tired, hurt, and sad… I am paralyzed by life.

I lie dying of a broken heart. My lips tremble,

"Help me, Lord. Time is short."

It always is. There is never enough time to bring to naught the past.

The future confounds what continence lies there.

How can it help?

Is it just another trap to confuse, sadden, and bewilder me?

Or is it a chance, a gift from God, to not right the wrongs of the past, but to live a precise life for Him and Him alone?

PART 4

Short Stories

No Destination
A Short Story by Matthew Cooke

There is nothing like the sound of tires humming on the highway, thought Randy. It was time for a road trip. Sometimes you must get out of the endless monotony of home. Not to mention the fact that is where all the demons are. You just think sometimes if you could put a couple of thousand miles between you and them, then everything's going to be all right.

Yes, this was one of those times. With no destination, a little money, and a lot of beer, the cosmos should shake some; but that proverbial worm must turn my way at some point.

Cruising down old I-20 does have a hypnotic effect on the cerebral part of my being. If I concentrate hard, I can enjoy the grandiose scope of the world going by. It is sequential, so I can make some linear sense of it. The beer just acts as a catalyst for me to keep my mind free.

The only problem is the leaving, the driving, and the drinking do not always help. Like a flash, a meteor of the past will run through my mind; and I will be there in that place, that moment of time, with nowhere to go. On these occasions—and there are many—it matters not whether it is a good recollection or a gut-wrenching, hair-raising one. They both immerse me in a fear that siphons out my breath and freezes my soul. *Time for another beer. All right, that's it.* These past visions can be good or bad, yet the effect on my psyche is the same.

There will come, at times, slow-moving meteors that flash and glitter. These will bring before my eyes times spent with my family picnicking on a spot picked out just for us by God Himself. Portraits edged into stone weigh heavily on my soul. A family with such love for one another that it saturates the air with incense and oil. The love, the tragic love—that is what I remember. As the thought leaves my orbit, its tail momentarily remains, leaving tears for times lost. I burn with rage for those clean, cool droplets of time, when the world was as it should be, and I knew happiness like I would not know again.

Another meteor crashes straight through my forehead, nearly turning my head and blinding my eyes. These space rocks are black with rigid sides and prickly fingers that dissect and destroy whatever they hit. I am cognizant in an instant what this time trash represents. It is a time when I lied, hurt those I love, and made my God cry. The distorted visions on the face of these hell rocks bring me back to reality, and I turn around and go back to where I came from, my place of happiness—home.

The Exodus

Long ago, before time was marked by human hands, there lived a great cascade of the most wonderful Flowers. They reached west to the Great Sea and east to the Pond, which would one day be their demise. These magnificent Flowers flourished in their lands, taking only what was needed to live. The Flowers ranged in the millions and although quite different in minute ways, were able to love and war and find peace again.

They knew God, for He lived among them and through them. They knew He was as close as the highest bush or tree. Glory, sadness, and sometimes death would wilt the Flowers; but the field of beauty that surrounded them and love for one another would carry them on.

On a day that was inconsequential, just average and happy for the Flowers, the Great White Cloud and a warm breeze began to blow from the east. Their brothers, the bear, beaver, hawk, and hare, felt the breeze and saw the White Cloud but did not know what to do—just as the Flowers didn't. The storm slowly made its way to the first of the Flowers in the east. These were the Mountain Flowers that flourished in the flora and fauna of the hills. These Flowers, like so many others in the land of magic and fertility, loved their home in the gentle green waves of the smoky hills.

When the Great White Cloud ascended upon the Mountain Flowers, they welcomed the Cloud to their meadows, hollows, and peaks. Their benevolence was unbounded, and the Flowers were happy to share the abundance of what they had. However, at some point, the Great White Cloud changed.

The Great White Cloud became self-indulgent and wanted all that the Flowers had. The Flowers of the hills could not fathom this. The Great White Cloud arranged for the Flowers to be moved so they could have the hills and the beauty and the air and the trees where God lived.

The White Cloud uprooted the Mountain Flowers and took them far from their home. The move was laborious for the Flowers, for they were in unfamiliar soil and alien lands. Many of the Mountain Flowers that partook of this trip lost their roots, then their petals, and then died a death far from their home.

The White Cloud found a land for the Flowers. It was a dirt unlike the Flowers were familiar with, a land flat and devoid of hills and mountains. It was a harsh life for the Mountain Flowers. Once the White Cloud had put the Mountain Flowers into a governable garden, the White Cloud decided it needed more of the Flowers' land, so westward it went.

The White Cloud was by now an immense storm that roared and ravaged through miles of the Flowers' land. They came to the plains of this rarity of a world, and the warm breeze of the Cloud was apathetic to the beauty of the land and skies. They heeded not the majesty of the Flowers they were killing and made them abandon their homes.

The White Cloud appropriated whatever it needed and then even more than that. The Flowers of the plains could not understand such thinking and greed. For the White Cloud took their sunlight, which nourished them, and even took their water, which strengthened their roots.

Alas! The Plains Flowers could not hinder the Great White Cloud from pushing even further into the Flowers' majestic land. The White Cloud contin- ued westward, worried about nothing but self and profit. It passed over the mountains that had many rocks and in so doing, left many of the Flowers' forest and mountain friends dead behind it. The Great Cloud passed the mountains to the deserts and found Desert Flowers there, but these Flowers fared no better against the Cloud. The White Cloud, at long last, came to the shore of the Great Sea and looked back over the land to the Pond from which it came, and the Great White Cloud was pleased.

Today, there are still places you can go and find the beautiful Flowers of this land. They are small points on the compass, but you can find them. These Flowers are not as abundant as they once were, and their ways of growing and living have changed. But their petals are still radiant and proud. So if one does decide to seek out the Flowers of this land we now call America, remember that you are seeing the true beauty—and God is just over the nearest tree.

In remembrance and reverence for the indigenous people of this land.

Matthew

The Gift

On a special day, one like another, I happened upon a box. It was wrapped and bowed most aesthetically pleasing for one such as I. The box sat alone. A queer spectacle to see a box such as this. A present really should have a tag, an owner if you will. Should it not be surrounded by others of its kind?

Being me, just a man, my interest was piqued. Thus, I circumnavigated this treasure, inspecting all sides, top and bottom. Completing my inquiry, I found nothing amiss. Further, I sensed to be drawn to the box by a force that was not of me.

Upon more reflection on my newfound treasure, I became quite obsessed as to its contents. Thoughts of riches and fame flashed through my brain. As my investigation intensified, I became acutely aware of my surroundings. A curious sense came upon me—I was "paranoid" that my plum may be claimed by another passerby. So I being me, a man in need, did then decide to sack the plunder for myself.

Heedfully, but with nothing else to do, I sat in proximity to the focus of my interest. Taking my time was a simple affair, for I am old with nowhere to be and even fewer that would wonder of me. After a considerable time, I made my move of stealth. My bones screamed foul as I lifted this vessel of flesh and walked (or merely shuffled) to what was to be my new magnificent future.

With the gift of my salvation straddled between my legs, I nonchalantly bent to claim it as my own. With the crinkle of paper and swaying of bows, I lifted this God-sent endowment.

Feeling free from prying eyes, I felt my heart beat as though I had just stolen the Hope Diamond. I thought, *Oh, finally success!* The ticket to my future was secure under my coat. I turned to stray away, making an expedient yet leisurely exit from the "scene." However, when my old yellow eyes scanned the route of my retreat, I became half entranced by a chilling premonition. This gift was not alone—it had a mate; it came in a pair! For there so obviously yet inconspicuously lay another box.

This box, though dimensionally the same, was indeed very different because it was plain. Caught unaware by my new find, I found myself at a loss as to my next endeavor. I, being me, did not want to leave this new morsel, even though it was in quite disrepair. Thinking for a moment longer, I made haste with the second box as well.

Losing my coat and tossing it over a chair, I made haste to my meager kitchen. There I ceremoniously sided my bounty upon the breakfast table. Giving both objects a fast eye of inspection, I left them there to begin my supper and change my clothes.

Living alone for as long as I have, one tends to become a creature of habit. Sleeping, eating, leaving the house, watching television shows, and even relieving oneself, all become as regular as the tides.

Humming is one of those habits I have unconsciously done while busying myself around the house. I'm usually unaware of the tune; tonight, however, I found myself humming the theme song to *The $64,000 Question*. I can't imagine why!

With a sly smile painted on my face and a light step (on a gimp knee), I fluttered, cleaned, shaved, and went back to my kitchen. Yes, there, still on the table as I had left them were the two perfectly symmetrical, yet uniquely, motley pieces.

With supper pouched away in an ever-increasing tube around my waist, I sat quite contented staring like a child at my newfound catch. A glow of anticipation engulfed me as I hypnotically perused one and then the other.

My initial appraisal was quite correct: both boxes were the same size, but one was prettily wrapped while the other very drab. However, now with time, good lighting, and defogged spectacles, I was able to see how truly ornate the wrapped box was. Its wrapping was more like a cover; it flinted with gold, silver, and pearls. The bows were of silk and beautifully displayed. The thought arrived to me that the box itself was very much a treasure being just a box. Thus, I reasoned, the contents must truly be otherworldly. In contrast, the poor battered box was fit for the refuge pile. It had the look of long neglect with its dents, footprints, and smudges galore. Heaven only knows why it was still intact, much less why I had lugged it home.

Glancing at one and then the other, I began to experience the strangest phenomenon. My hairs prickled, and a sense of foreboding covered me like a fog. Fire and ice seemed to simultaneously emanate from the forms on the table. The forces seemed to acknowledge each other as they seeped from their seams.

I was at once terrified and mystified, and my thinking spun on a whirlwind of wild ideas and grandiose conclusions. "Get ahold of yourself," I muttered. I stood to gain some control over my mental faculties. "These are merely lost presents—gifts for children, no doubt," I said aloud. Standing back, I took a deep breath and decided that some cocoa may be in order. With cocoa in hand and night winds rattling my panes, I sat and stared at nothing at all. Why I did not just throw caution to the wind, tear open the sash, flip up the lid, and solve this mystery before me, I do not know. But I being me hunched on my chair and did what I did on all solemn nights.

Like a worn and well-watched film, my past sprang to vivid life before my eyes. Oh, the times I had, had! Youth was so fleeting, gone in a flicker of a sunset. *Why had I not relished it more, seized each day as it was the last?* Now, all alone, memories are my soul companion.

I recalled the good and the bad I'd experienced—the mother, the father, the brother, the wife. I had known love and hate. I had worked and lived, drunk and eaten. I had sinned and repented a thousand times over. Yes, I had lived a thorough life. A typical life, I would say. I had made no real marks but did little harm. It all seemed so mundane, so pointless to me now as I waited impatiently for death.

Ashes to ashes, dust to dust… Is not that what they say? Ha! There will be no mourners for me, no wake, no procession. No, not one ever to care. It will have been as though I had never lived. "So be it!" I raged. "Is that so unlike any man's life?"

Well, there it is in a nutshell, I thought, coming out of my reverie. "Oh, no matter!" I shouted. "On with the show!" Did I not have two presents before me? Maybe they would be the answer to my woes.

Dawdling no longer, I reached out and slid the ornate box off the table. Caressing it in my old lap like a shield, I closed my eyes and wished for wishes to come true. Like opening an oyster to find a pearl, I gently began to remove the bows.

Oh, how my broken heart fluttered as the silk streamed to the floor in a dance of red! *Now the top! That was all. Just rip it off, look inside, and then claim your "just deserves."* My gnarled hands shook as I lifted the lid.

The container opened with a hiss. The pungent smell of sulfur stifled my senses. Dropping the lid, I staggered backward, hacking and wheezing as I went. "What on God's earth could this be?" I demanded. "Something dead?" As the air thinned to a tolerable level, I anxiously crept back toward this conundrum upon my table. Holding my breath and squinting my eyes, I lifted the cryptic gift and peered inside.

"Oh, dear God!" I squawked, as the contents became clear. For the inside was full of the blackest of black. Death itself loomed from within. I stood frozen in terror as the consummation of a lifetime of sins enveloped me. It was all there to see! Every sin of my life, the horrid acts done in secret, came vividly to light. The vortex of darkness gleefully mocked me as I writhed in guilt and shame. As the darkness slowly overtook me, the torture was unbearable as my being screamed for clemency. But there was to be no reprieve, no pardon for me.

For an eternity (it seemed), I stood there convicted. My eyes lay dry; there was no tear left to shed. Damnation beckoned me, and I was alone for the call. I balked. *I could not go! Please not I!* Oh, for this wretched box—this horrid life I'd lived—I deserved eternal hell for the man that I was. But mercy, O mercy, take this thorn from my side!

Though I knew I stood guilty of all I had seen, I wanted to deny my sin, which was ingrained in me. For I wasn't a fiend.

"By chance or by promise, might there be another way?" I bellowed. At the end of my wits, my torn and tangled life, my stone-turned heart, and my lusterless eyes, I acknowledged the fate of my doom.

A glimpsed memory flashed before me. In the midst of my deranged madness, I recalled the other gift. What a hoot! Though I was dying, morbid fascination guided my corpse to grasp the battered box. "Maybe this will be death itself," I crazily cried, "an end to the waiting!"

Filled with self-loathing and hopelessly lost, I threw open the top of this poor neglected box. My mouth hung agape, my heart in my throat, as I waited to be swept into hell's ghastly gates. But, alas, nothing happened! No deadly serpents sprung, no bomb exploded—my heart did not even stop. "What is this?" I demanded. "More tricks of the devil just to taunt me a final time before his eternal talons tear into my flesh?"

With a myriad of feelings (all of them bad), I tilted the box over to discern my fate. "Oh, Lord,"

I said softly seeing the gift. For there on the bottom, lying all by itself, was a plain wooden cross. Perplexed and badly shaken, I reached inside and gently clasped the cross in my hand. Feeling the wood and seeing the shape, I began to remember what this symbol really meant. I fell to my knees as if struck by a hand. I knew in that instant what I needed; it was so obvious, so deceptively easy! I lay with my nose to the floor. Then with all my strength, all my heart, and all my mind, I began to pray to Jesus:

> "Jesus, I believe you are the Son of God. I confess that I am a sinner in need of your forgiveness. I believe that you shed your blood and died on the cross to pay for sins. I ask you to forgive me and wash away my sin with your blood. I choose to turn my back on my sinful ways and renounce the works of evil in my life. I choose to follow your path the rest of my days. O, come into my life, Lord. Fill me with your Spirit, and be my Lord. In your Holy name, I pray. Amen!"

Suddenly, I was standing, and energy surged through my being. It was as though I was newly born and the world around me had metamorphosized. Trying (in vain) to clear my head, I laid the holy cross on the table between the two boxes. When in a brief moment before my awestruck eyes, the blackness, the sulfur, all the sins of my life, and yes, even death were mystically drawn into the cross. As the light of righteousness shone through the room, I was again overwhelmed by the glorious truth that Christ Jesus had won, victorious over all the evil that plays havoc with us. He is the Way, the Truth, and the Life.

He was indeed my long-awaited *GIFT*.

The One That Got Away

It does not take much to make a memory… It could be a ball hit out of the park when you were thirteen; a sunrise watched with adoring eyes with your first love; or just a beaten-down, rocky path making its way beside a cold mountain stream. Yet these are the memories that lift our hearts for a lifetime and are never forgotten.

In the annals of my deepest heart, with just a tinderbox and spark, I can conjure many of these uniquely human and spiritual highs. With just a small emotional push, I recall one such path next to an exhilaratingly cold yet soul-cleansing brook. Through the fog of time, I see two small figures emerging from the smoke of my mind on that very path. As these young boys walk into my mind's eye, through blinding sunshine and dark shade, suddenly, like magic, there I am walking beside my best friend, my brother.

I cannot be sure of the exact day or even year; but that is of no consequence, for it is eternal. We stride side by side, not alone because a great number of other tourists were around, yet we were by ourselves. Carrying our Zebco poles and brown plastic tackle box (filled with only hooks and Niblets whole corn), we were lost in the conversation, laughter, and love of little boys.

The sights and sounds of this two-mile hike are frozen in my mind as much as my mother's face or my daughter's. For we were not part of the tourist horde that made this ascent, these were our trees, our rocks, our river, and yes, our trail. Only a short way up, we simultaneously look right at Tom Branch Falls. Very seldom would we stop and gaze; the point was it was always there—always would be for us. As the flora and hardwoods, rhododendron, ferns, and flowers passed us on each side of our journey, we talked. Just talked.

We spoke of fishing and our cunning technique. We spoke of lightning bugs, swings in the hammock, bike riding, and girls. But most of all, we spoke with no regrets and no anxieties for tomorrow. The foreigners in our realm floated down the stream to our right then, after crossing the first bridge, to our left. Our feet were as light as monarchs' as we ascended to our swimming hole. We glanced over but moved on, not because there was no huge trout—there were just too many people... always too many people.

I have always thought it humorous yet touching how humans tend to attach their own names to objects that are not theirs. Yet when we become connected, become intimate, we very often do. That was why we now were walking up "Cardiac Hill," the steepest part of our journey. However, our lungs did not strain, and our legs did not hurt—but our souls soared. The ravine down to our creek becomes quite steep at the crest of "Cardiac Hill". Here we did finally stop, not to rest but to look down upon our river.

Fifty feet below, through the trees, we watched the water and the people floating down it. Our point of interest and amusement was the "Washing Machine" (our name, of course). It was a smallish three- to four-foot waterfall set between two enormous boulders. As aesthetically pleasing as it was, our real glee came from watching rafter after rafter—man, woman, and child—completely wipe out. What more for a boy than to watch the mishap of others!

After a few laughs and talk of our attempts on the Washing Machine later, we once again continued our journey. Not far up the trail from our brief interlude, just to our left, at the beginning of a short pathway, stood a sign. It was only three feet tall, made of wood with carved out letters. We passed it without notice. There were only five words carved on this small sign; however, through a lifetime of reading, I will never forget those five words: "No tubing beyond this point."

The sign was situated at its coordinates so the river upstream would be preserved in its natural state and its pristineness would not be altered by people. However, inevitably it did change, as all creation does. Yet for my brother and me, from that sign onward, our creek had been—and always will be—the same since it made its first cut down that mountain.

Soon after the sign, our pathway forked to the right and to the left. Being astute and experienced fishermen, we took the left fork and thereby crossed our second bridge. Not far along, a transition was made; it was not perceptible by us, but it happened just the same. Our chatter was minimal, our mouths shut, and our ears blossomed like petals of a daylily. It was not that we had nothing to say; yet now, truly alone, we listened to the sounds of a world that enraptured us.

The stream was louder now, the rustlings and scampers in the woods reverberated in our heads.

Our eyes became astute to all movement. We were in our wild place, our *wonderland*. Could that scamper beyond our sight be a deer? Could the small movement of a bush be a snake slithering away? Or possibly, without a sound, could a black bear step from the darkness of the forest and cross our path? Of course, we did not know, but we hoped—oh, how we hoped! And that was the excitement, the allure.

Walking carefully yet not cautiously, we rounded the next bend, coming closer, always closer, to our destination—perhaps our destiny. Our trips were less about fish, I think, but more about our ability to accomplish. The fish was our trophy to bring back to Mom and Dad, showing them and ourselves that we could.

As I reflect back now, years later, I believe that we as children of God spend a multitude of time doing this very thing. Yet back when innocence engulfed us like a sea, it was about the fish and the fishing; and most of all, the comradery of brothers, God, and His astounding creation, we strolled through. I wish I knew as a man, as a human, how to hold onto that unblemished part of the soul that somehow dies as childhood withers away. But on this day, just two lighted souls walked this trail, and that is what life is really about.

We were approaching our hallowed fishing ground, the third bridge. There were small chutes and eddies where we would apply our trade. The creek was narrow here but had shallows as well as depths, with rapids forward and aft. Our strategy was a simple one. First, we would stand on the short wooden bridge with two small handfuls of corn. Second, we would throw the corn upstream into the slower moving water. Third, we would watch intently as to where the rainbows and browns would dart from their hiding places to suck in the corn.

I feel inclined to digress briefly to explain why trout would be so adamant about wolfing down Niblets corn. The answer is a simple one: the trout mistakenly believed the corn kernels were fish eggs. That is why fishing with corn in these waters was illegal, but legalities meant nothing to little boys on a great quest.

We would then divide our forces—going this way and that, standing on one rock or another, upstream or down, in the water or out—trying to gain the best vantage point possible. For now, the competition began with vigor. If you have ever fished, you realize it involves 99.9% waiting and 0.1% pure, unabated excitement. And that was what we spent hours waiting for: that 0.1%. I must again digress at this point because again, I antiquate much of fishing to life.

We seem to spend the vast amount of our time, from birth to death, waiting, maintaining, and going through the motions until we reach that climax, when we experience those few moments our world explodes. It happened to me when my eyes met my wife's, when my first daughter was born, and when I knew Christ was my Savior. I am sure you have had that 0.1% part of your life as well, and that makes the rest worthwhile.

Well, on this day, under the third bridge up Deep Creek Trail, my brother and I had our 0.1% four times. We caught four exquisitely wonderful rainbow trout. The only rub was we had no stringer to bind the fish so we could keep them in the water (thus alive) without them getting away. So I, being the oldest, devised a way around this conundrum. There was a small two-yard-wide estuary that ran into Deep Creek. I built up a circle of rocks to hold the fish inside, a fish jail cell if you wish. It was a masterful idea and worked quite well. This way, we could continue fishing with no worries of our captives getting away. And that is exactly what we did…for a while.

However, life is life; and just when the world is seemingly your oyster, tragedy strikes. While I was skillfully luring my prey to one side of the stream, my sibling was on the other side traversing the bank when I heard an "Oh no!" I instantly focused my attention to the voice and saw my brother standing by our "jail," tears in his eyes. The rock that was the cornerstone of our incarceration was gone.

Along with the rock being gone, so also were the trophies our prison once held. I waded the creek with speed to see if I could recapture at least one runaway con, but to no good end. I was furious while my brother was crying, and there we stood in our transcendent kingdom; mad, hurt, and humbled.

Finally feeling magnanimous, I put an arm around my brother, my best friend, and said, "That's all right, Bo-Bo. We'll catch them again." Those few words ended our day of fishing, and we started our descent back to camp empty handed. Yet we were young and in love with each other, the world, that creek, and those hills. Before we were halfway back, the chatter and laughter had returned; and all was forgiven but never forgotten.

I do not know if through the years we ever caught any of those same four rainbows again. But I like to think they are still there swimming those waters, bigger than any of their peers, telling the story of how they got away from two fair-haired boys. Yes, those fish got away that day, but the memory for me never will. I pray yours never will either.

PART 5

Faith

Comforting Waters

I see beauty all around me, a cascade of life and wonderment and awe. When the winds whip the leaves in autumn, when the birds sing in the spring, and when the greenness of summer surround me, I am in love. Life is like a torch set on fire—it radiates, it lights the way, it reaches out to touch and sets ablaze those that are around it. It attracts, yet it also destroys. Our hearts on fire are such a primal entity. They can love, and they can hate; they can be broken, yet they can mend. It is what pulls us to our true desire, our pleasure, and sometimes our pain.

The heart I seek is not troubled or disturbed; it's not doubtful, resentful, or full of wrath. My heart is an angel ready to spread its wings so that I may soar over the pain and anger and enlighten on the truth and happiness of love and the bounty of the blessings that have been bestowed upon me by my Maker.

My memory is elegant. It is a mirror that shows no blemishes, yet it is a world I cannot escape! The past blooms like fragrant flowers but soon wilt into the reality of my presence. I swim in a river of time that does not flow, one in which I cannot swim forward, backpedal or tread. As I look down on the glassy waters of my life, I see a myriad of images that evoke such happiness, such longing, such hope, and yet such unrelenting pain. The souls that swim in my waters of life bring smiles, tears, and a fear that is incalculable.

When the reflection ripples and breaks, I can only see my face upon the teardrops that ripple the spring water of my life. When the raindrops from my eyes cease to fall, when my life's stream becomes smooth and mirrored, and when my soul becomes at peace, I will be happy again! I am haunted by the waters. Yet I awake each day yearning to see the calm, clear, cool waters that comforted me as a child. How I long to be that child again! But this time as an adult with the waters calmed and cooled by another Father, who is in heaven.

I travel along a wave of time; friends, loved ones, familiar faces glide by like the clouds of the sky. Some change with the blowing of the wind, others disappearing completely. I sometimes marvel at the new manifestations that I see materialize in the heavens. The world and the universe are ever changing with a beauty so intense that our eyes fail to see it. Sometimes our view of what are the truly important, lovely, and consoling aspects of our lives are skewed and shaded by the busyness, by the self-absorbed, worldly activities we become bogged down in. I have found that when I let go of the world around me, I can then, and only then, start to appreciate the wonderments of life.

Life is a blessing that should never be taken for granted. Life should be savored in one's mouth, in one's soul, and in one's heart like the juices of the sweetest fruit—of the most loving thoughts, the warmest feelings, the most joyful sounds of heaven. My being cries out for that freedom and joy. I exist only for that day when the lights of wonderment, beauty, and wisdom are bestowed upon me once again.

My mind's eye soars through the past like an eagle looking for the most filling meal. I fly though the amber waves of the Midwest, through the mist of the Smoky Mountains, through the rainbows of every cascade I have ever seen. There is never a shadow cast over my memories, over my soul, or my beliefs in the wonderment of life. But yet I am wanting! The darkness of my physical body envelops me. It is a strangling force that is unjust, unrelenting, and incapacitating.

These black chains can be broken, and I can soar again. They can be busted and ground to dust by something as simple and beautiful as a rainbow. Glory to all of God's promises; with them, we can ride the colors of the universe to a new freedom, to a new tomorrow, to a fabulously eternal life in the kingdom, where the clouds are our footrests and rainbows are our slides.

The past lingers like a fog in front of my eyes. I am aware that it is gone, but the mist of it still obscures my vision of the future. I can recount so many virtuous moments in my life, moments that brought glee, moments that were awe-inspiring, moments of tears and happiness; but more than any of my recollections, I remember shame and doubt.

I have seen the sun glisten through leaves of gold, yellow, and orange. I have witnessed wind-swept plains that are beautiful in their bearings. My eyes have seen sun gleam off glaciers that are as old as time itself. I have been lifted by the beauty God has spread over the corners of the earth. Yes, I have seen these images, these wonders; and I have been brought to my knees in tears by the astounding aesthetic and spiritual greatness of this earth.

Yet I look inside of myself; and I see a void, a place of darkness and sadness.

I know not where these feelings emanate from, for gladness and joy have always surrounded my life. I was born Matthew, "a gift from God"; and I know that somewhere deep in the contours and angulations of myself, I can bestow these gifts to others and become a complete man.

Matthew

Daily Prayer of Psalms

Father, I come before You in the name of our Lord and Savior, Jesus Christ, thanking and praising You for this day. For this is the day that You have made, I shall rejoice and be glad in it. I thank You, Father, that You have given me this day; and I enter Your gates with thanksgiving and into Your courts with praise. I give You all the glory and the honor, and I bless Your Holy name.

Father, You said that if we acknowledge You in all our ways, You would direct our path. Father, I acknowledge You in all my ways concerning this day, and I thank You for directing my path in every situation. Father, You said that if we commit our works unto You that You would establish our thoughts; so, Father, as I commit all my works unto You, I thank You for establishing and directing my every thought throughout this day. Father, I pray that You would be a lamp unto my feet and a light unto my path today and guide me with Your eyes and Your spirit as You order my footsteps.

Heavenly Father, You said that You desire above all things that we prosper and be in good health, even as we would prosper spiritually. I pray that You bless me to prosper in You spiritually as You bless me to draw nearer to You through Your Spirit and Your Word. I pray that this day, I will come to know You more and draw closer to You; for You said that if we draw close to You, then You would draw close to us.

I thank You, Father, that my soul searches for You this day. I thank You that I am blessed and prosperous in my health, finances, and in every other area of my life. I thank You, Father, for my health and that I am continually healed from the crown of my head to the sole of my feet and that Your healing virtue flows through me continually; therefore, by the authority of Your word, I confess that no plague, sickness, or any spirit of infirmity shall come nigh my dwelling because by the stripes of Jesus Christ, I am healed.

Father, I thank You that You are my Shepherd; and as my Shepherd, You said that I would have no need of want because You promised to supply all my needs according to Your riches in glory through Christ Jesus. You promised not only to supply them exceedingly abundant but even more that I could ever ask for or think. Therefore, I praise and thank You, Father, for meeting every need in my life this day and every day—whether spiritually, physically, or financially—and for Your abundance in every area of my life.

Father, I thank You for the hedge of strong and mighty angels which You have set around my family and me, keeping us safe from all hurt, harm, and danger, spiritually as well as physically. I thank You that they watch over us, protect us, and fight for us.

I thank You, Father, that no weapon that is formed against me shall prosper and every tongue that rises against me shall be condemned. I thank You for rebuking the devourer from every area of my life for my sake. Father, I pray that Your power and anointing be so upon me that when the enemy comes against me one way, he shall be forced to flee from before me seven different ways.

I thank You, Father, that Your Spirit goes before me this day to make all the crooked things straight and the rough areas smooth. I pray that every trap the enemy would set up for me this day would back-fire on him and work out for my good and Your glory, for You said that all things work together for good for those who love the Lord.

I take authority over the devil, every demonic spirit, every principality, and every spirit of wickedness in high places. I bind them from my life this day and from the lives of my family. I render every demonic spirit against us helpless, powerless, ineffective, and inoperative to prosper against us in any way. Satan, you are under my feet. I pull down every stronghold, and I cast down every wicked and demonic imagination in advance. Satan, I command you by the authority of the name of Jesus Christ that you lose every hold from my life and to touch not one of God's anointed.

I thank You, Father, for giving me the mind of Christ. I pray that the spirit of the Lord rests, rules, and abides upon me this day with a double portion of Your anointing and power; and I pray that the glory of the Lord shines bright in my life. I thank You, Father, that the words of my mouth and the meditation of my heart be acceptable before You. I pray that You set a watch over the doors of my lips and bless me to guard my heart with all diligence by the discipline of my eyes and members of my body.

Father, I present myself unto You this day as a living sacrifice. I pray that You bless me to live holy and acceptable unto You, which is my reasonable service. I thank You that I will not be conformed to the world or the world's way of thinking, but rather transformed unto Jesus Christ by the renewing of my mind in Your Spirit and Your Word.

Father, I pray that You help me to walk in the Spirit this day, as well as every day; for You said that if we walk in the Spirit, then we will not fulfill the lust of the flesh. I thank You, Father, that I walk not in the lust of the flesh but rather in the power, might, and strength of the Holy Spirit. I depend upon You wholly to keep me and sustain me. I also depend upon You to help me walk in the victory that Jesus Christ has already given me; and I pray that You lead me not into temptation, but deliver me from every evil and demonic temptation and snare of the enemy.

Father, I pray that You give me favor with those who are in authority over me. I pray as I go to my job, those over me will be well pleased with my work. I also thank You for a good working relationship with others I work with, as well as those who work under me. Father, I pray that throughout this day, You bless me to let my light shine before those around me that they will see my good works and it will glorify You, O Lord.

Now, Father, I thank You for giving me this new day as a day of victory, power, strength, and prosperity; and I pray for Your will to be done in my life this day as Your will is done in heaven. Father, I rest in confidence this day knowing that if You are with me and for me, which I know that You are, then nothing is strong enough to come against me and succeed. I, therefore, have a confident and great expectation that You shall take me through this day in victory. So I say to God be the glory for the things You have done, You are doing, and shall continue to do in and through my life this day and forevermore. In Jesus Christ's name, I pray. Amen.

Mathew

Flame

My life began as a smoldering ember. The heat of
the smallest heartbeat rose from the ashes.

Then from the void, like the clap of a bolt, a tiny
flame flickered; and my eyes beamed for the
first time.

The light of the Lord started my life and fanned my
soul, my body, my mind.

He gave me the food I would need to grow. I
received the guidance for all the knowledge I
would need to know.

Somehow though, along the way, my spark broke
free; and I started to fade.

The winds of time and the heat from below altered
my being and changed my life's flow.

Though my Father's love has never failed to exist,
and I realized He is there and begging to assist,
I turned away.

My fuel is depleting. I feel it slipping and passing
faster each day.

God, how I need You. I don't want to go, so I pray
this prayer though I feel so low.

"Father, please bless and give me faith because your precious flame is not ready to leave this place." Amen.

Glory of the Dance

God is good all the time. Yet I fall woefully short. My joy has slithered away like a serpent, careening away, and with it my el vital. Come back, snake! I implore you. Come back.

I am reassured that this dandyish void of pain will end one day. Without that innate faithful assurance, I would become helplessly impotent in this life.

Through God's help, I will emerge on the other side, scathed and hurt but *alive*. Glory!

Then the night may return as a peaceful escape from the day...

Then, only then, will the katydids and frogs surround me at dusk, laboring in unison to bring an enlightened orchestra to my ears. Then the music and dance will be back in my life once more.

Glory, glory...

Jesus the Blanket

The Lord Jesus is like a blanket to a small child... whether it is hot or cold, a child always covers himself with a blanket while he sleeps. The blanket gives the child a sense of security; it makes him feel safe from the evils of the outside world. When the child is frightened, he covers his head and trusts the blanket to keep him safe.

The Lord Jesus is much like the blanket. If you cover your soul with Him, you will feel secure and safe. When you are scared, He will protect you from the evils that scare you. So all you must do to get this secure and full feeling is to trust Jesus Christ as much as the young child trusts in his small but meaningful blanket.

Matthew
Age 10

Life

Have life before death. Do not yield what is yours;
   your dreams, goals, ambitions.
Carpe diem!
Seek the life you were rewarded. Do not quit!
Fight the noble fight; be brave, strong, and endeavor
   to persevere. Fear not, not even fear itself.
Know that the Lord created you, watches you, and
   loves you.
If the bowels of hell rise up to meet you...smile.
Be glad of heart; stand with the knowledge that the
   Son stands with you. Be thankful! Accept your
   plight, your talents, your deficiencies.
Whatever you do, seek life before death.

Linguist

I am surrounded by a world of beauty and unfathomable contrast. Overwhelming is this sphere;
I twist and turn like a white flag in a gale.

How can I relate to this place or antiquate it to you?
I am not a lyricist for this planet... I am only a
journeyer.

The flora and fauna evoke a tapestry of images and
emotions. I float through the artistry of time,
spellbound and mystified.

My time is short—just the blink of an eye. I feel it
in my soul; my spirit longs for freedom.

Words fail to describe my existence; I am lost in a
translucent landscape of madness and bliss.

From whence I came, I do know; from whence I
am going, I am assured.

I was born to blood, and it is *Holy* blood that will
birth me again.

My solace is in Thee; my tears are for those that are
lost.

May I stay upon the narrow path with Your light as my feet's lamp.

Matthew
March 30, 2007

Man's Time

"Haven't you ever been there?" said he.

"No, not I," he said.

"Would you like to go sometimes, maybe with me?" said he.

"No, not I," he said.

"You will never know unless you go," said he.

"Perhaps not," he said.

"Time is short. Don't you want to know? Don't you want to go?" said he.

"Not yet," he said.

"The possessions you will gain will be immeasurable, if you will only go. Follow me. Make haste," said he.

"Not yet," he said.

"The earth shall be yours and all that is in it. Your Father will tend to you personally. Don't you want this gift? Don't you want your Father's love and adoration?" said he.

"I guess, but not now. Not yet. In a bit," he said.

"Oh, friend, don't you know our Father's time is his own? Come now and join your brothers, for you will be sorely missed," said he.

"He shall wait for me," he said, "for Father loves me."

"Truer, you could not be. However, the Father's time is short. And those not with Him are against Him, loved or not," said he.

"I have but little more to do, small tidings to gather in, then I shall be ready for the Father's call," he said.

"Hello," he said. "Hello," he said. "HELLO!" he said.

"Goodbye," said he.

Once upon a Time

A crystal of eye-sparkling brightness slivered its way into the colorful slit of the blinds.

This minute prism of wonder and promise manifests itself from interventions outside the realm of our true understanding and begins and ends with the Breaker of the Night.

"How can this be?" say we, for we were at the end. None came after, like none has ever come before. The end is most certainly the end; but as you are there, be always aware. For some will find through the darkness of *end* a small guiding portal of time.

Following this light will sometimes be frightening and often overwhelming. Stand fast! Have the faith of a mighty warrior. Believe in yourself and the Breaker of the Night. Do this, O journeyer; and a wonderful spiritual metamorphosis will take place cloaked in the armor of salvation, righteousness, truth, and faith.

Matthew

Poem of Prayer

My heart pulsates inside a prison of bones. The
soul of a martyr beckons to be free.

A valley of skeletons dangles like a grisly vision
before me. Ravens are consumed with the mor-
sels of my flesh.

Rains cannot quench my thirst; the sun will not
warm me. Arctic winds freeze my blood. I
shiver, petrified.

O Abba, Abba…send the east wind to cleave the
sea set before me.

Lead me from defeat, O Lord! Guide me to the
glory that is found only in You.

Wings of fear flap against me. I am affixed by this
world. Deliver me from my tormentor; sever
these chains of death that bind me.

Keep, O God, my consciousness on heavenly dwell-
ings. Release thy wisdom upon me.

Let the clamor of earthly knowledge give way to
Your awesome wonder.

Here I am, Father. You see me from afar humbly
making my way back. Please rush to me, Father.
Smile, embrace, and kiss me. Dress me in Your

finest robe, and kill the fattened calf... For I was blind, but now I see; I was lost but now am found...

I love You. I am coming home again. Amen.

Matthew
December 2003

Second Birth

I awaken to a warmth that is all about me. Though I am conscious of myself, I remain in the half dreams of sleep. Every side of my sleeping room feels soft and warm upon my current delicate skin. Through this semi-conscious exploration, I realize I want for nothing... I am in concordance with my body, mind, and spirit.

Just as all goodness comes to an end (which I did not at the time know) external forces began to intrude upon my tranquility. Meddlesome figures from a world that transcends presumption begin to talk, tap, and grope at the folds of my domicile.

Finally, forces outside of the realm of my control conclusively decide that my works are in the world of the living, not of the immature nature of man that heeds not his mind or body to it.

I am called forth from my glorious tomb of tranquility, surrounded by faces that are both recognizable and foreign. I fear but am not afraid. I feel the resurgence of the moment, the day, and am pleased.

I am fully awake now, born to a new day—a day birthed from God to me. It is now up to me, O Father, to give You Your daily gifts of birth by being obedient to You and serving Christ through the birthday gifts You have given me.

The New Beginning

I am cloaked in the armor of faith, love, and works.

You, my love, will ignite the night with dazzling,
radiant light.

In the clarity of this light, the realization of *the end*
being but an illusion is exposed.

The end is found to be but a waystation hurtling us
into the most exciting, soul-lifting, gratifying
part of our life... The new beginning.

So now, my fellow travelers, I say to you farewell
and Live happily ever after...
The end

Where Is God?

Is He at work or at play through the hustle and bustle of every day?
"Yes." But you don't talk with Him even though He
   walks beside you.
Is He at your home as you walk and roam through
   all your rooms and down your halls?
"Yes." But still you don't see Him or take the time
   to look and find.
Is He there in bed when through all your thoughts
   that you remember and say, "Oh, and God,
   while you are on my mind and I have the time,
   I would like to thank you for this day"?
Where is God? He is everywhere—at home, at
   work, at play; throughout the hustle and bustle
   of every day. You just have to see Him and talk
   with Him.
He should always be on your mind, and you should
   always have time for God.

(Matthew wrote this when he was nine years old.)

Because of the LORD'S great love we are not
consumed, for His compassions never fail.
They are new every morning; great is your
faithfulness, I say to myself, "The LORD is
my portion; therefore I will wait for him."

—Lamentations 3:22–24 (NIV)

About the Author

Matthew was born in Columbus, Mississippi, but at the age of three moved to South Carolina, where he became a true South Carolinian. He loved the beach and South Carolina football. Matthew was an avid reader, traveler, and sports enthusiasts who loved his family dearly.

In 1997, Matthew graduated from Coastal Carolina University with a bachelor's degree in education. He also attended Tennessee Tech University while working on a master's degree. He loved teaching all ages—from children to adults. Matthew's love for God, family, and nature is evident in the writings he has left as part of his legacy to his family and friends. Matthew went home to be with the Lord he loved on November 3, 2019.

CPSIA information can be obtained
at www.ICGtesting.com
Printed in the USA
LVHW011353310821
696551LV00001B/31